Sally Swain was born in 1958 in Sydney. After taking a BA in psychology at Sydney University, she travelled Europe and has subsequently worked as a freelance illustrator. Her bestselling *Great Housewives of Art* was published in 1988.

By the same author

Great Housewives of Art

SALLY SWAIN

GREAT HOUSEWIVES OF ART
Revisited

Grafton

An Imprint of HarperCollins*Publishers*

Grafton
An Imprint of HarperCollins*Publishers*
77–85 Fulham Palace Road,
Hammersmith, London W6 8JB

A Grafton Original 1991
1 3 5 7 9 10 8 6 4 2

A catalogue record for this book
is available from the British Library

ISBN 0 586 21394 5

Set in Perpetua

Printed in Italy by STIGE Turin

INTRODUCTION

You see me, but you don't see me. I am everywhere,
but nowhere.
Who am I?[1]

I have been painted over and over,
as madonna, virgin, mother, wife;
as temptress, witch, monster;
as goddess and passive nude love-object.

You see me. I am everywhere.
Painted in stereotype. Projected male fear, desire, fantasy.

But you don't see me. I am nowhere.
I am invisible as subject.
My experiences, feelings, ideas, activities – invisible.

I am invisible as domestic labourer. My care of man, child,
environment – life-sustaining, but unseen.

I am also invisible as artist. My expression has been
diminished, overlooked, suppressed. Sometimes my work is
claimed as his work. I do the work; he gets the credit. He
creates high art; I dabble in the minor arts. He is artistic
genius; I am mother and wife.

You see me, but you don't see me. I am visible, but disguised.
Who am I?[2]

I paint, I write, I parody. I do not alter prints of famous
artworks – I reconstruct them and paint each and every
brushstroke, using the language of great artists.

Here, I strive to re-draft art history; to paint woman
into the picture.

You see *me*. *I* am everywhere.
Who am I?[3]

I am experiencer, senser, acter, interacter.
I do ordinary things – I scrub, queue, park the car.
I do extraordinary things – I perform miracles,
create the Universe.
I cook, clean, support, nurture, make things nice.
I love, share, struggle, forget, relax, get fit, get angry,
get aware, take control.

Here I am.

1. I am the image of woman in art history
2. I am Sally Swain
3. I am a Great Housewife of Art

ACKNOWLEDGEMENTS

Thank you to Mum, Dad, Jen and Stu for their sensitivity, support, encouragement, brilliance, astute suggestions, ruthless criticism and most of all – love.

Thank you to my friends for their warmth, closeness, respect and for being there – in particular Estelle, Barbara and Stefan for help with words and photography.

Thank you to my agents and publishers.

For Iris, David, Jennie, Stuart
and the spirit of my grandmother, Millie

GREAT HOUSEWIVES OF ART
Revisited

Each Stone Age husband must engrave
and paint a bison in his cave.

This prehistoric Altamira
rock art draws the dinner nearer.

Stone Age housewives can divide
and cook the bison with this guide:

Be lavish with the herb and spice on
Number One – scrag neck of bison.

Wise and thrifty cave householders
stew cut Number Two – the shoulders.

Simmer well to best digest
cut Number Three – the flank or breast.

The belly, Number Four, you braise
and serve with mammoth mayonnaise.

Cut Five, most choice from bison plump,
is grilled as juicy loin or rump.

And Six, the leg, you barbecue
with dash of totem and taboo.

They cook by numbers with a chart
that's functional, but *is it art?*

PALAEOLITHIC
COOKING GUIDE
after cave paintings at
Lascaux, France and
Altamira, Spain,
c. 15,000–10,000 BC

When seized by gastronomic wish
that grows into a craving
for char-grilled kangaroo or fish,
consider microwaving.

Avoid 'old oven' stigma
and the slowness of combusting.
New ovens have enigma,
plus more buttons for adjusting.

The how and why of microwaves
continues to perplex.
This oven, *some* believe, behaves
by beaming Rays of X.

The X-Rays also function
as a style of art. You view
the guts, without compunction,
of a see-through kangaroo.

You close a door, a tray revolves —
entrancing carousel.
But everything alive dissolves
in organismic hell.

Fans stir, autos defrost, you touch
controls for who knows wattage.
Tradition rich is lost within
the electronic cottage.

This intelligent appliance
your recipes remembers,
but you leave your self-reliance
in glowing fireplace embers.

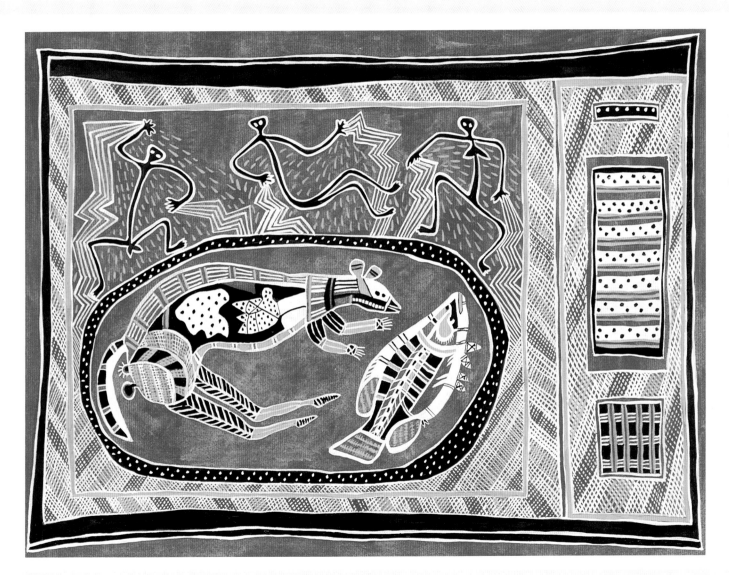

**MICROWAVE
DREAMING**

after Aboriginal Australian
traditional rock and bark
paintings, *c.* 40,000 years
ago–present day

We old Egyptian postal workers
serve with sideways smile,
our eyes and chests in frontal view,
the rest in strong profile.

If you wish to buy a stamp
or post the Sphinx a riddle,
all Kingdoms will be catered for –
the Old, the New, the Middle.

In place of ritual offerings,
why not employ a drafter
of arty correspondence for
a soul in the hereafter.

A telephonic telegram's
not visually terrific.
You may prefer a pictogram –
come in and hire a glyphic.

For those environmentalists
of envelopes desirous,
we use recycled, safe, bio-
degradable papyrus.

All packages should indicate
their contents with description
like 'Cleopatra's deadly asp –
it's ancient and Egyptian'.

And if your mummy's Heaven-bound
in ugly old pyjamas,
please call our special mail-room staff
who double as embalmers.

IN THE POST
OFFICE JUST
BEFORE
CHRISTMAS
(3 weeks BC)

after Egyptian
tomb paintings,
c. 2000–1500 BC

BATTLE OF THE SEXES CLASSICAL KNITS

Knit your husband a toga in the latest sixth century BC
up-to-the-minute designs — 'Athene slays Enceladus',
'Hera strangles Zeus' and 'Psyche confronts Eros'.
There's nothing spartan about these ideal knits of
Truth, Beauty and Simplicity.

Tension
Carry out a tension check
before commencing
garment.
If your knuckles are
white, you are too tense.
If you drop your spear,
you are too relaxed.

Knitting abbreviations
K = knit
K2tog = knit two togas
P = pose heroically
sl = slip
st = stumble
sp = spear (him *now*, or
you'll be ancient history)

Yarn quantities
Colossal

Measurements
Olympian

Instructions
Mythical

**ATHENE KNITS
A TOGA**

after Greek amphora
painting of Athene slaying
the giant Enceladus,
c. 6th century BC

QUETZALCOATL PHARMACY CONTRACEPTIVE AND PARTY GOODS SALE

Our astonishing range of contraceptive devices double as party entertainment aids.

1. *Condom or Raincoatl*
   For safe xex. Optional quetzal feathers.
   Also use as balloon.

2. *Xintrauterinals*
   Moderately ineffective and quite unsafe
   a) *Coil*
      With ring pull. Now available in jaguar
      or ocelot skin.
      Also use as firework.
   b) *Pretzelcoatl*
      Pull string in case of human sacrifice
      to sun god.
      Also a savoury party snack.
   c) *Snake*
      Poisons unwanted sperm.
      Also functions as bottle opener.

3. a) *Cap or Ovacoatl*
      May leap across room if not controlled.
      Also functions as headwear.
      Use in conjunction with:
   b) *Contraceptive jelly*
      Which also makes a tasty dessert.

4. *Pill*
   28-Dot calendar-friendly contraception. 98%
   effective. Contra-indications include nausea,
   loss of libido, giddiness and death.
   Also use as candy.

5. *Multi-function Super Gadget*
   Chops, dices, slices, purées, peels, stops
   pregnancy and takes out the garbage.
   Also mixes a mean cocktail.
   Effectiveness: none. Safety: none.

pharmacy

WHICH
CONTRACEPTIVE
DEVICE?

after Mixtec *Codex
Zouche-Nuttall*,
Mexico, *c.* 1400

SWEEPA

Goddess of Housework and Purity

Legend has it that Mukna the Filth Monster tried to overpower Sweepa by living everywhere that humans trod. He created a land mass of rotting vegetables, toenail pickings, industrial refuse and teapot mould.

But Sweepa grew two extra arms. She turned the sea into foaming laundry detergent and mopped and dusted and scoured until the world was gleaming once again.

However, now that she had started cleaning, she could not stop. Unbeknownst to Sweepa, her jealous husband Opresh, God of Business and Enterprise, had cast a spell. He wanted to ensure Sweepa stayed home and didn't go off to university where she would learn about the world, become dissatisfied with her lot and meet a nice, young, educated, virile god. So Opresh decreed that once Sweepa began cleaning she would be doomed to eternal housework. If ever she abandoned her duty, Mukna the Filth Monster would swallow up Sweepa and then the entire world.

That is why, to this very day, Sweepa and her daughters and her daughters' daughters wash and polish and wipe and scrub eternally, endlessly and forever.

AN INDIAN
GODDESS'S WORK
IS NEVER DONE

after Indian miniatures,
c. 18th century

1. Pour 6 cups cold water into medium saucepan.

2. Gently stroke face and body of lover. Add small amounts scratching and biting.

3. Bring water to the boil.

4. Pour 2 cups rice into boiling water. Stir with chopstick.

5. Partially remove kimono. Allow him to caress your body. Sigh sporadically.

6. Yawn daintily while entry takes place.
   Remain demure.

7. Turn down heat. Simmer for 20 minutes, stirring occasionally.

8. After climax, clean up mess.

9. Drain and serve.

THE ART
OF JAPANESE
EROTIC
COOKERY

after Japanese woodblock
prints, 18th century

PARTY MIRACLES AT MAGIC PRICES

Trick	*Cost (in gold coins)*
loaf – white	2
– wholemeal	3
fish – dead	5
– alive	6
water to lemonade	10
water to wine (adult parties only)	15
walk across swimming pool – kiddies' pool	20
– Olympic	25
disabled to able-bodied	30
blind to sighted	35

HOUSEWIFE'S REVENGE

Her husband's bathroom rituals
were more than she could bear.
He squeezed the toothpaste from the top
and caked the soap with hair.

The hair was of the pubic kind –
curly, black and short;
a paradise attracting germs
to revel and cavort.

His soggy towel adorned the floor
entwined with dental floss.
A fungal jungle filled the bath.
The shower sprouted moss.

The toilet seat stood vertical.
Its lid stayed upright too.
He splashed with yellow pungency
and *never* flushed the loo.

By unhygienic conduct she
was driven to distraction.
Spurred on by slime, she found the time
to launch a plan of action.

She baked a casserole of hairs.
His towel she dropped in bed.
The toothpaste tube she filled with glue.
They are no longer wed.

IF *ONLY* HE WOULDN'T LEAVE THE LID OFF THE TOOTHPASTE

after Cross Page from *Lindisfarne Gospels*, Irish illuminated manuscript, *c.* 700 AD

HASTINGS HYPERMART CAR PARK

Fees
- First 2 hours – free
- 3rd hour, or part thereof – one suit chain mail
- 4th hour, or part thereof – one suit chain mail plus one Norman (conquered)
- Over 4 hours – one suit chain mail, one Norman (conquered), an arm and a leg.

Rules and Regulations
- Validate your shield
- Overtake other drivers – or they'll beat you to this week's specials
- Remove spears from shopping trolleys before returning them to Bayeux
- Tether horses, anchor and lock ships.

Proprietor not liable for injury, loss or damage
(with exception of arrow through eye) to any
person or vehicle, notwithstanding any act,
omission or attack on the part of the Proprietor.

- No oath-swearing permitted, Harold excepted.

WELCOME T O hESTINGA hVpE R MART : hAVE A NICE DAV

THE BATTLE
OF HASTINGS
HYPERMART
CAR PARK

after the *Bayeux Tapestry*,
embroidery, *c.* 1080

Instructions follow here, describing
how to change, with honour
and reverence, a nappy soiled by
offspring of Madonna.

Inhale at risk of spoiling your
expression sweet and tender.
Disgust or even faint distaste
are not on the agenda.

Get talcum powder, bucket,
nappy fresh and safety pin.
Wash hands to stay immaculate
of concept and of skin.

Now, call a band of angels
for, unless you're fond of scandal,
certain things, however holy,
icons must not handle.

**MRS DUCCIO
CHANGES A NAPPY**

after Duccio di
Buoninsegna's *The Virgin
and Child with Saints
Dominic and Aurea*,
tabernacle, *c.* 1300

Mrs Giotto, housewife and mother of at least six,
heralds the new Halo dish-drying method:

'You can't do better than this glorious technique. It's
fast, efficient and stacks of fun for the whole family.

I used to dry up alone and be constantly drained.
Now I've discovered the Halo method – a real blessing.

No longer do I urge the children to help with the
dishes. After dinner they soar from the table, wash up,
place crockery and cutlery on their angelic
little heads, and take wing.'

MRS GIOTTO
PREFERS THE
HALO METHOD
OF DISH DRYING

after Giotto's *Nativity*,
fresco, Arena Chapel,
Padua, 1302–5

TV PROGRAMME

Paradise Channel

6.30 'Expulsion from Eden Street'
(soap opera) (repeat) (Parental Guidance)

Tonight's episode:
Mr and Mrs M commit dreadful,
although quite original, sin.
Mrs M forgets to collect laundry.
Hapless couple parade naked
through neighbourhood, wearing
nothing but badly painted foliage.
The Masaccios banished forever
from Eden St.

Next week:
Mrs M begets Cain and Abel.

MRS MASACCIO
FORGOT TO PICK
UP THE LAUNDRY

after Masaccio's *The
Expulsion from Eden,*
fresco, Brancacci Chapel,
Florence, *c.* 1427

MEN!

You can change the world by changing yourself.

And the only way to change yourself is by eliminating womb-envy, through

CO-BIRTHING.

In Co-Birthing, a simple technique, a man simulates pregnancy and childbirth.

Enrol in a day workshop or weekend intensive at the World Co-Birthing Centre *NOW*.
You will find the Co-Birthing experience fulfilling and amazingly regenerative.
You will enjoy a great release of tension followed by profound calmness and well-being.
Connect with your inner power source and tap into blissful cosmic peace.

Testimonials:

Mrs van Eyck, Ghent, Minnesota:

'We found the Co-Birthing experience both exhilarating and challenging. At first it turned our lives inside out, but now my husband is glowing with a love and serenity beyond belief. He is kinder, more compassionate and even helps with the housework!'

Crystal Rune, Fairyland, California:

'Unbelievable!'

MRS VAN EYCK
SHARES THE
BIRTHING
EXPERIENCE

after Jan van Eyck's *The Arnolfini Marriage*, 1434

Mantegna paints me pierced and martyred.
Sewing's not for folk faint-hearted.

Markings on a sewing pattern
look like Greek to me. Or Latin.

Needleworking, I'm not nimble.
God! It's torture with no thimble.

Wholly, I atone for sins
by cushioning these neat new pins.

My body's punctured. Just like Saint
Sebastian. I feel quite faint.

Darned bloody wounds! How I must suffer!
Roman martyrs were much tougher.

I meditate on how I'd feel
if stretched like Catherine on a wheel.

I'm relieved, though life's no lark,
I wasn't burned like Joan of Arc.

Stitching I can't cotton onto.
Maybe I don't really want to.

MRS MANTEGNA
CAN'T SEW

after Andrea Mantegna's
Saint Sebastian,
c. 1455–60

BREAST EXAMINATION
FOR NEWBORN ROMAN GODDESSES

Examine breasts regularly for abnormalities.

1. In the shower. Hover on Neoplatonic designer shell. Look weightless.

2. Tilt head slightly. Look translucent.

3. Clasp exquisitely long golden hair, decorously covering pudenda. Look ethereal.

4. Adjust hot and cold taps to zephyr-like spray. Look sweet and graceful.

5. Keeping fingers together and flat, feel breast with gentle, circular motions.

6. Repeat with other breast by swapping hands, at no time revealing mound of Venus.

7. Always remember you must simultaneously idealize both Classical love-goddess and Christian madonna.

MRS BOTTICELLI
EXAMINES HER
BREASTS ON THE
FIRST DAY AFTER
HER PERIOD

after Sandro Botticelli's
The Birth of Venus,
c. 1480

MRS DA VINCI'S FANTASTIC WEIGHT LOSS STORY
(or 'Now I fit into the Slim-Trim Hoop of Perfection'):

'I used to be overweight, listless, about 57 years old, 4'10" in height and a horrible 102 kilos – not a pretty sight. Enough to make that Mona Lisa smirk.

Since attending the Ms Universe Slim-Trim Weight Loss Clinic I've become a slender, perfectly proportioned 22-year-old Renaissance beauty. I've grown several inches in height and I take an active interest in aeronautical engineering, astronomy, philosophy, dissecting cadavers and inventing things. Last Supper, Leonardo and I invited twelve guests. We served Slim-Trim lo-cal bread and wine. Divine.'

MRS DA VINCI
LOSES WEIGHT

after Leonardo da Vinci's
*The Proportions of the
Human Figure*, 1485–90

Before

After

Poor Micky's bending over backwards,
hanging, lying, kneeling.
A genius with aches and pains, he
decorates a ceiling.

With artists' wages meagre,
chiropractic bills galore,
I'm forced to trudge the skies to
sell cosmetics door-to-door.

While Micky's working overtime
embellishing the Chapel,
I tempt and lure with Eve Nite Creme
and Scent of Adam's Apple.

For skin possessed by evil acne —
Blemished, scarred and spotty,
those pimples can be exorcized with
Cleanser Buonarroti.

I've Genesis Foundation for
a born-again complexion
and Essence of Creation gives
celestial perfection.

Six days a week Mick paints and I
press doorbells. On day seven
we stay in bed, ignore the kids —
a working couple's heaven.

**MRS MICHELANGELO
SELLS COSMETICS
DOOR-TO-DOOR**

after Michelangelo
Buonarroti's *Creation of
Adam*, Sistine Chapel,
1508–12

'I've been meaning to defrost the fridge since the Renaissance, but kept getting sidetracked.

First, Rembrandt wanted me to pose as Potiphar's wife, then Susanna with the Elders, then Bathsheba and God only knows who else.

We had the Reformation and the Counter-Reformation.

Then we had to have lots of boring Puritans and rowdy Cavaliers over to dinner. *So* much cooking.

Then we fell on hard times when Rubens was doing soft-porn pictures like *Rape of the Sabine Women*, which spoiled the market for sensitive, humane portraits of mistresses.

Well, I've finally got around to defrosting the fridge.

Can't let it wait till the Enlightenment.'

MRS REMBRANDT
DEFROSTS THE
FRIDGE

after Rembrandt van
Rijn's *Woman Bathing*,
1655

In the beginning was the Sink. And the Sink was Shiny.
And Mrs Blake spake unto her daughters.
And she saith:

'Every silver lining hath a cloud.
And the cloud must be scrubbed. Only New
Miracle Kleenbrite penetrates the heavens,
spiriting away dirt and grime.
Go forth and sterilize, my children.
For the squeaky-clean shall inherit the earth.'

MRS BLAKE
WORSHIPS NEW
MIRACLE
KLEENBRITE

after William Blake's *The Ancient of Days*, metalcut with watercolour, 1794

The work of Jacques that all revere
is neoclassically austere.

While I indulge in my ablutions,
Jacques paints oaths and revolutions –

compositions noble, bold,
but boringly precise and cold.

Jacques' réalisme is pedantic.
Je préfère un homme romantic.

Jean-Paul Marat – il est mon cher.
We're having une petite affaire.

While in the bathtub I relax
Marat declares his love by Fax.

Luxuriating in the tub,
I find some dark red stains to scrub.

My pleasure's ruined by this chore.
What *is* this mess upon the floor?

Mon dieu! I see that blood was shed.
Marat, my hero, are you dead?

YOGA SANITISSANA OR 'DOMESTIC YOGA' ...
is Yoga for Health, Beauty and a Sparkling House.

Its repetitive rhythms reflect the endless circularity of housework – sedating, meditative.

The yoga posture (asana) of *Nookancrannasana*, commonly known as the *Duster* or *Spineless Twist*, has many benefits, e.g.

- provides good stretch for the back
- keeps you supple and spongy
- helps you reach those hidden crevices that gather dust

Instructions
1. Start with cleansing breath to rid yourself and your house of impurities. Remember, *in*hale beautiful fresh disinfected energy and *ex*hale toxins.
2. Entwine legs.
3. Place right hand on left upper arm.
4. Place left hand on right thigh, or is it left?
5. Slowly twist spine until looking self-consciously over right shoulder towards viewer.
6. Inhale. Dust. Exhale. Dust. Inhale. Dust. Exhale. Dust.

MRS INGRES
ENJOYS THE YOGA
OF DUSTING

after Jean Auguste
Dominique Ingres'
Odalisque, 1814

'Joseph and I have just been through a stormy patch. He gets caught up in a swirling vortex of work. So tempestuous. This morning he tried to lighten the atmosphere with breakfast in bed. He's a real Romantic at heart. Of course, he burnt the toast. What can one expect with a *man* pitted against the element.

Smoke everywhere. I was fuming.

Must stop gasbagging. It's full steam ahead with the chores.'

MRS TURNER
EMPTIES THE
VACUUM CLEANER
after Joseph Mallord
William Turner's *Steamer
in a Snowstorm*, 1842

'OK – welcome to Wednesday Gleanaerobics.
We're here to work out and GET FIT. Right hand
to the ground …
Yeah! … Flex those biceps … Grip those
handweights … ooh … feel that terrific stretch …
That's it … capture a bit of that "hero of the soil"
flavour …
Come on, girls, see if you can strike a monumental
pose against the flat, dull landscape and glorify even
the humblest rural folk …
Tighten those buttocks, pull in those tums …
and bend and bend and glean and glean …'

MRS MILLET
ATTENDS A
FITNESS CLASS
after Jean François
Millet's *The Gleaners*,
1848

Neighbourhood Watch is loads of fun.
I ogle, peer and peek
at B-grade dramas starring all
my neighbours, through the week.

I have no need for video.
I unplugged my TV.
Each morning I just hoist the blind
to see what I can see.

Young Mrs T's a prostitute.
Her granddad deals in dope.
The kiddies gamble on the dogs.
Who needs a boring soap?

I like domestic violence.
A slap, a scream, a bruise,
a good old wallop in the jaw's
more shocking than the News.

Of bedroom antics neighbourly
my eyesight never wearies.
I wasn't quite as satisfied
by any mini-series.

This show has universal themes.
It's riveting and timeless.
I hope I never move into
a neighbourhood that's crimeless.

MRS WHISTLER
PARTICIPATES IN
NEIGHBOURHOOD
WATCH

after James McNeill
Whistler's *Arrangement in
Grey and Black No. 1: The
Artist's Mother*, 1871, and
*Symphony in White No. 1:
The White Girl*, 1862